PRAY
TELL

PRAY TELL

poems

Charnjit Gill

atmosphere press

Published by Atmosphere Press

Cover design by Matthew Fielder

Atmospherepress.com

A Message from Charnjit

In its essence, this collection is about the oneness of creation, eternal divinity, and how that transforms over time, including us in the process. We as human beings want to reach the depths and heights of our human potential by pursuing our passions and turning them into strengths so that it's considered inspirational. Knowledge is cognition but spiritual evolution is recognition where you hope to reach oblivion. The process is mesmerising, especially when you can see beyond the physical. When the human psyche meets the divine, it is a profound, sublime, and sacred experience where the destination is serenity. This is me attuning to universal wisdom, following my intuition, and being my higher self. Honouring the voice within clarifies things you don't hear. This is living in a prayer. Everything can be faith, but nothing is scripture.

This book is my way of acknowledging divine intervention and honouring it. I'm not saying having faith makes all your problems disappear or that you don't experience any pain. I'm saying that my faith has given me the psychological and emotional strength to deal with life: to heal. This is going beyond my mind and excavating my soul. It's my way of talking back to God. Faith can seem unreasonable or even audacious, but it doesn't mean you don't stop and wonder 'What is God doing?' Lapses of faith are part of the process, you can be blessed and lost. Sometimes we are stagnant in the dark but are led by light. The glory of God drives the desire for devotion.

Throughout the book, I use the term 'God' but please feel free to substitute this to something that makes you feel more comfortable i.e. 'deity', 'supreme being', 'divine', 'lord' or 'Universe' or 'soul' or 'beloved' or 'higher conscious' or anything else. Maybe Godliness is having multitudes of oneself. As if I know.

Every time I had a crisis of faith, I questioned it, but along the way, I ended up strengthening it.

I hope you never lose your appetite for miracles.

I'm not trying to get a message out; I'm trying to get the message in—in your head, in your heart, and in your soul.

I'd like to dedicate this book to people who are humble in their aspirations, gracious in their success, and resilient in their failures.

If anyone has had to be strong, if anyone has felt heavy but empty...

This book provides a comforting place. This book knows loss and feels your pain. This book sends you love. This book is a shoulder to cry on. This book will find ways to hug you. This book is both long and short because life is both long and short. It's a matter of life and death. The gap in between is love.

This is for you...

I hope you find solace in it.

Contents

Action

Wake Up 3

Faith and Principles 4

Stop picking up what God is telling you to put down 5

When 6

Blessings 7

Sincere Sins 8

Calling 9

Trust 10

Patience 12

Job 13

Honour 14

Gift 15

God's Development 16

Catch Blessings 17

Faith 18

Pray 19

Forget 20

Plans 21

Decisions Prayer 22

Mute Prayer 24

Message 25

Answers 26

Incoming 27

New Leaf 28

Bring in God 29

First 31

Knowledge

Image 35

Voids 36

Custom-Made 37

Blessed 38

Coherence 39

Rock 40

Hope 41

Purpose 42

Faith 43

Spiritual Evolution

Spiritual Evolution 47

Repentance 48

Talk to God 49

Believer 50

God's Voice 51

Believer 53

Prayer Fix 54

Dealt 56

God's Lessons 57

Distance 58

Situations 59

God's Work 60

Worry 61

Nothing 62

Tears 64

Heaven Opens 65

Cry to God 66

Redundancy Prayer 67

Find 68

Footsteps 69

Surrender 70

Trust the Process 71

Correction 72

Strength 73

Empowered 74

Disrupt 75

Preparation 76

Spiritual Stamina 77

Strongest Warriors 78

Spiritual Training 79

Grace

Grace 83

Mould 84

God's Hands 85

Imprint 86

Pleasure 87

Blameless 88

Silent Prayer 89

Quality Control 90

God is Good 91

Blessings in Disguise 92

Miracles 93

Abundance 94

Meet 95

Lonely Place 96

You 97

Put Myself Out There 98

God's Plan 99

Bump 101

Catch 102

Provide 103

Truth

God's Dream 107

Expression 108

Pronunciation 109

Cuckoo Clock 110

Count 111

Mystery 112

Sarcasm 113

God is not a vending machine 114

Enlightenment 115

Gratitude 116

Holy Rebel 117

You are waiting for you 118

Inconvenience 119

Rest in God 120

You 121

Action

Wake Up

Sometimes there are days that you are woken up because God is
thinking about you
You wake up blinking
Your third eye starts winking
You might have an inkling
But it'll take a while to sink in
Every day is a new beginning

Faith and Principles

Sometimes you can cling to your faith
Your principles
Your values
And still fall out of line
Fall out of favour
With what you want
What you need
What you think you deserve
Naturally, it becomes a concern

Stop picking up what God is telling you to put down

It's not a clown's magic trick
This is how your crown slips
The let-down makes you feel rundown
The comedown can lead to a meltdown
So before there's a showdown
Just shut it down
Before you break down

When

When you pray, God listens
When you listen, God talks
When you believe, God works
When you're good, God gives you perks
When you're in darkness, God sends fireworks

Blessings

The problem with blessings is that you try to measure them
Through success, material possessions, health, wealth, happiness
and intellect
Instead of treasure them
Then with each blessing, you expect something better
But a blessing is God's goodwill gesture
It's asking for a favour
Or protection
Hoping that by getting a blessing you're more worthy of
acceptance
It's the acknowledgement of a sacrifice
Or an excuse for God to make up for what you lack

Sincere Sins

I walked the road with nothing but my sins and my sincerity
I learnt that people won't pray for you
I learnt that you could quote chapter and verse and it'll still hurt
I've learnt that you can breathe deeply and your heart will still
burst
I've learnt that you can be first and still feel last
I've learnt that God could be a better doctor if you were a better
nurse
I've learnt that people count their blessings like they're directly
proportional to the contents of their purse
Still, it could be worse
I've seen so many blessings in disguise
That I thought it was a curse
Especially at first
Because you can make it happen for other people but not yourself
Like you weren't God actualised
God manifested

Calling

What if I told you that destiny was chasing you?
Fate is following your footsteps
Looking out for your luck
Making sure you're getting exactly what you want
What you need
What you're dreaming of
Greatness wants to grab you from the shoulders and say 'I got you'

Trust

God gave you time
But He didn't give you a watch
So watch yourself
Keep an eye on the time
You don't know how long you've got

Trust God's timing
Even if you're crying and you get tired
He's fighting for you
When you've lost yourself
He's finding you
When you're in darkness
He's shining
When you've lost meaning
He's defining
When you're not expecting anything
He's surprising

You wait
You pray
Sometimes you get frustrated
You'll ask questions
But you'll be patient
Continue waiting
Continue praying

Then one day, it'll take you by surprise
It will happen
Keep believing
Trust God
Trust His timing

Trust God
Put prayers into action
When you feel abandoned
See that as advancement
Use it to your advantage
For your enhancement
It's all in your understanding

God gives you a timeline
It's up to you to make it timeless
There's a fine line
Between timely and in your own time

Patience

Do not rush what God is taking time to prepare
He's heard your prayer
But what He's creating for you is rare
People want to climb up a ladder but forget about the stairs
When things go wrong, we swear
But when things go right, it can't be compared
So don't despair
Not all bad dreams are nightmares
Not all paths lead to dead ends

Waiting on God is hard
Wishing that you had waited on God is even harder
Let faith be your armour
Don't despair
Partner with prayer

When everything is too much to bear
Patience shows that you care
Patience makes things fair
Patience makes you aware

Job

Loving God is a full-time job
With many duties and responsibilities
Payment is in blessings
There are lots of perks
But it's worth all the hard work

Honour

Sometimes I imagine how God feels when He sees you doing the
right thing, knowing it wasn't easy for you
But you chose to Honour Him
That's a hymn in itself
When you follow your inner compass

Gift

God gave you a gift
A talent
A skill
Don't let anyone talk you out of using it
You don't want to lose it
So infuse it with your intuition
You can't misuse it
It'll reduce its value
So keep trying
Keep it moving
Scoop it all up
Illuminate it
Raise the bar again
Achieve maximum impact
Express it
It's better to—
Otherwise it'll be left inside of you

To use the power that God gave you isn't arrogant
It's common sense
You're doing what feels natural
With elegance
The excellence becomes evident
That's what makes you hesitant
You become your own medicine
Always relevant

God's Development

Let them underestimate you
While God develops you
God takes you to the next level
So doubts fall away like petals
God will let you revel in Heaven
Let you settle there
It's angelic
While others get jealous
But people can be petty
While you're growing
Let them be embarrassed

Catch Blessings

Let your hands be so busy catching blessings
That you don't have the capacity to hold onto grudges
But who are we to pass judgement on others?
Sometimes trying is rolling with the punches
At least you're touching the pads
To create a different kind of percussion

Faith

Sharpen your faith
Hone in on it honestly
Listen to improve your intuition
Blunt belief
Fine-tune your facts
Perfect your passion

Pray

Sometimes you need to pray into your own ear
Just so you can hear yourself

Forget

Sometimes forgetting mistakes is a relief
Forgiving someone
So that the hope can come back to you
Accept that is the way things are
Let go
It's a different chapter to the story
Have faith in the universe
In God
Everything that is lost will be replaced
But you don't find it right away
Keep going
Something better is on the way
Detach
Love yourself

Plans

They say if you want to make God laugh then tell Him your plans
But since I don't make plans
I guess the joke is on Him
Since he designed them
He programmed the project
A blueprint with a strategy
The masterplan of you

Decisions Prayer

Dear God,
I make difficult decisions based on faith
I trust that when you entrust me with something
I might struggle a little bit in the beginning
But eventually everything will be alright.
This is you
All you
I don't make plans
You'll only make it better
So I might as well
Let you do your thing
Like you haven't already
I will adapt to the way you shape me
Everything is a reminder of what you've taught me
And what I value
Anyone or anything that was removed from my life is because it's
not worth what it used to be
If anything, at all
Thank you for ensuring that I didn't bend to the will of other
people
Only yours
When I'm wrapped in your presence
Chaos seems calm
Because your leadership and guidance encourage me to follow the
path
Something about you strengthens me

I've seen the darkest roads and felt relieved when others would be
scared
There's a peace in pitch black that you can't find anywhere else
But you made it that way
The weight lifts
The divine defies doubt
Resilience made me recover faster
There is serenity in hardship
It transformed me
When others called me fragile
You gave me stability
Growth is sacred
When you know who is behind it
Thank you for continuing to try
Even when I didn't want to
The best thing about being torn apart isn't being stitched back
together again
It's realising that I was seamless in the first place

Mute Prayer

God doesn't shout
He whispers
But you need to stay close
Stay silent
To listen

There is power in the mute prayer
Because God still hears
Still bears your burden
God knows that you're scared
That's why you shared it with Him
Don't compare yourself to others, you'll only despair
That won't get you anywhere
You must take care of yourself
There's so much up in the air
There's so much you're unaware of
That's why God always handles you with care

Message

There will be a clear message
An instruction
It will be obvious
Easy to understand
You will have faith in it
Because it is what you have been patiently waiting for

God will speak to you through other people
Dreams
Music
Listen
It closes the distance
It keeps you driven
It seems like fiction
But it's fixing problems
That can be a given
For all the effort you've put into achieving goals
Learning lessons
You are living minute by minute
To the story you've written
Breaking the condition
Of making decisions
Listening to opinions
But give yourself permission to follow your intuition

Answers

Trusting God means that you acknowledge that you don't have all
the answers
As long as you keep asking questions

Incoming

Dear God,
I'm on the way to you
I've already made this trip thousands of times
But this time I'm going to stay
Break away from life
Run away from reality

New Leaf

I've turned over a new leaf
Over and over again
Faith is foliage
But the canopy is character
Truth from an everlasting tree

Bring in God

Bring in God
Usually at the last moment
He always comes back
Lay out a table and chair so He knows where to be seated
Place food on the table so He can eat
Once He's eaten
Ask your questions
All of them
You hear the answers
Life spread out in front of you
Are you surprised?
To see your own life
We are inside of it so we can't see it
There's no shape
Nothing like it
Especially since everyone is so different
We have not seen it grow the way we do
It has changed
It's undeniable
But we're too close to it
We don't know where we are because we're always in a hurry
Even if we slow down, you couldn't tell me

We walk
We dress
To play the roles of our lives
We want to keep what we have
Maybe that's too much to ask
We are hungry for what we are becoming
Even if we don't know what that is yet

First

Put God first and you'll never be last
He'll give you what you need before you ask

Knowledge

Image

God didn't make you in His image for you to hide
God made you in His image to guide you
Back to yourself
Ride the wave
Don't be beside yourself
For not taking things in your stride

Maybe we weren't designed to be finished
Maybe that's the biggest lesson
Call me a cynic
We were made in God's image
But we got caught up in self-interest
We have our human limits
But we push it because we have God's spirit
Finishing is a mark of winning
But witnessing is just the beginning
When you're not finished, it doesn't diminish what you've
achieved
It distinguishes it
Instead of extinguishing it
We are always replenished

Voids

All sins are attempts to fill voids
It's harder to avoid
When the noise gets louder

Don't know what you're enjoying
Or destroying
Bu there's joy in it
That spoils us

Custom-Made

You don't worry about fitting in when you're custom-made
Your originality ensures that you don't fade
It guarantees that you make the grade
Being custom-made, it doesn't matter how much you're paid
But in life's game, it's more about how you played
How much you prayed
How many times you were a light in someone's life?
How many times you paved a path and strayed?

Blessed

You're too blessed to be angry
You're too patient for that
You're too blessed to be bitter
You're too content for that
You're too blessed to hold a grudge
You're too forgiving for that
You're too blessed to think about what didn't work out
Because too many things did

Coherence

Find coherence in chaos
There are times when the darkness seems endless
But the light is endless too
We get confused
Walking in between the two

Rock

God is the rock
We turn to Him when we're stuck in a hard place
Paper covers the rock
But it can't stop the power of the rock
We're constantly paper chasing
The paper covering the rock might be the blessing in disguise
Maybe God doesn't want to help us directly
So He hides
The scissors may cut you
But the rock will break the scissors
Rock is the foundation, but it's everything on top

Hope

Hope is a prayer
An expectation or a desire
Laid bare
If you dare to feel it
It can scare you
If it's not shared
Otherwise, there's despair

Purpose

God made you on purpose
With purpose
Just because you don't know what it is
That doesn't mean you weren't made purposefully
If anything, you were made multipurpose

Faith

I thought I got it
Faith, I mean
I've always had it
Grasped it
Right between my hands
But the truth is
I didn't

Bare feet that are keen to move
To walk
Down a path
Sometimes it takes you places you would never go
Especially on your own
That's what makes it a splendid idea

There's so much I don't know
There are so many levels and stages that I've never been
The glory is in the places in between

Spiritual Endeavour

Spiritual Evolution

Discipline is a spiritual evolution
Survival of the awakened

Repentance

We see people's sins but not their repentance
There's always a struggle for acceptance

Talk to God

I need to talk to God
But He's never missed one of my calls
But I think I've missed a couple of His
I'm too busy texting these prayers
Because the letters were never sent
Maybe this was the signal
When you're not in a hotspot, of course you feel cold
But the closer you get
The better the connection
I'm not checking the calendar to schedule a call
I guess that must be the perks of being eternal
It's alright for Him
He's sitting on a cloud
While I'm on the ground
I'm stuck in this matrix game
Where God decides how the values change
I've cc'd you on the email with the subject, "Are you still
watching?"

God's voice

Dear God,
Sometimes there are so many voices to listen to
All wanting to be heard
All saying different things
It's absurd
Walking by faith means following the direction and talking to
about it along the way
I've built my life
For you
So when they see me
They see you
Your love
Your light
Your healing
Your grace
Your peace
You

Black Holes

I filled the black holes in my heart
So that the constellations in my chest could shine
They did for a while
Only when I was aligned
Thoughts and emotions move with the tides
So I guess it was just a phase
I don't know what I was looking for, but I know that I didn't find
it
I wasn't looking for God because I already found Him
Somewhere between my intellect and my intuition
Right there in my heart
So whenever I needed Him, I took a deep breath just to start
Every time I said that I needed to get something off my chest
He put a pen in my hands
And held a mic up to my lips
I listened to podcast after podcast
Hoping I might hear it
Took the silence as a sign for as long as I could bear it
Listened to music like it was injected in my veins
Let the goosebumps and instruments take over instead
Let the words wash over me
I read book after book until I couldn't look anymore
Forget the cover
I don't judge any of it at all
I wasn't sure if I escaped or was imprisoned
When you felt that way for a long time, it's hard to know the
difference

Jails are subtle

Escape routes become detours or dead ends

So making it out alive really is the new making it

Everything has to be real

There's no faking in this

Half-baked dreams might as well stay as batter

If a cake doesn't rise, it may as well be in tatters

You're doing this for your sake

So you might as well give whatever it takes

I wrote and I wrote

Until I was lost for words

I watched documentary after documentary, knowing that you

couldn't document me

I watched film after film

But I only saw stills

I ate past hunger

I ate beyond being full

To satisfy the appetite of staying alive

Believer

Being a person of faith doesn't mean you don't feel isolated
Or afraid
Or lonely
Or purposeless
At times you do
At times you will
You ask God for guidance
And try to navigate your way through
There will be frustration
Especially when prayers are unanswered
But God is fair
There will be pain
But God will also pamper
At times you feel hopeless
But God will handle things He knows we can't
There will be doubts
But there will be more times that God saves the day
Trusting God doesn't mean you don't fail
Or that it's an easy path
You hurt just like everyone else
The only difference is that you've been hanging on to God's hand
for so long that you start to get the hang of it
And if you hang about long enough, you might just make it to
Heaven

Prayer Fix

Dear God,
Fix me
I think I'm the problem
Things fall away from me like leaves in autumn
Maybe I let go of things too easily
Or I hold on for too long
I don't know
All I know is that sometimes in spring
I don't always have something that blossoms
Unless you put the seed of food for thought
Because you reap what you sow
But I think I've got too many things in tow
I just want to see the fruits of our labour
Because if You're working on me
I'm working overtime
Starting from the bottom up
Because when my foundation is faith
The root of responsibility lies in me
So let me find solace in Your serenity
I won't wobble in the wind
I won't blindly follow trends
Just kept my heart full
But what can I do with all that love?
If I haven't got someone to give it to

So, I give it to You
To myself
My family
My friends
That's just me problem-solving

Dealt

God dealt you a hand for a reason
Don't try to fold
God made you warm
Don't try to be cold
God made you unique
Don't try to mould
You've got a lot to tell
Don't be told
God's got a plan
Don't try and control

God's Lessons

God's lessons are never over

God is making sure that you're not a pushover

So, He creates a scenario where He can empower you

The teaching creates closure

All of this will be added to life's folder

To remind you that you are the owner

God has a poker face

But we are posers

Pretending to be posters

God puts weight on your shoulders

To make you go slower or be stronger

But you must walk with composure

This is God's full disclosure

God is in the light

So you can get full exposure

Now lessons change things

They make you a different person.

Trust His plans

It adds up better

When you subtract yourself

Divide the responsibility

And multiply your faith

Appreciate the pain, setbacks, and delays

God always makes it worth the wait

Students wait for the teachers

For confirmation and approval

The most difficult exams mean more when God teaches you how

to get the highest score

Distance

If you feel far from God, who moved?
Who must prove themselves once again?
Who is going to approve?
Who said that God is so far removed?
Is God unmoved?
Whose ego is bruised?
Who should be excused?
God or you?

Situations

God will put you in situations with no information
So you have to make your own calculations
Once you realise why
There's a celebration
I'm sharing this for circulation
For education
Those situations provide elevation
In isolation
Meditation provides navigation for your spirit
It's only through observation
That the preparation is done

God's work

When I got made redundant, God really put the work in
So did I
I worked on myself
I became the clerk to my thoughts and feelings
Lurking over the words
I perk up with poetry
I don't shirk form work
But it's all about time like clockwork
Then the fireworks go off
When you spend your whole life trying not to put a foot wrong
You need to check your footwork
So you can create the right framework
For the groundwork to be done
It all feels like guesswork
It's a knee jerk reaction
To put in the leg work
But it's all God's handiwork
To make sure I'm not overworked

Worry

Dear God,
I'm sorry I worry sometimes
I know I don't need to worry
But when you get stuck, you start to wonder
But I know that this is the best position to be in
This patience is for my perseverance, character building, faith, and
providing me with I everything I need for the future you have
ahead
Waiting can make you impatient but when it's worth it (which it
always is)
It works out
When I'm not working is when you work the hardest on me
Sometimes you can have the all the weapons to fight and not the
strength

Nothing

Sometimes nothing makes sense
Let God help you
Enjoy the silence
Take a moment
Release the weight
Find strength in your vulnerability
Accept things as they are
Not as you want them to be
God loves you
Even if you think no one else does
That is more than enough
God will welcome you
When others will shut the door in your face
God comforts us in the way that we need
Not by the people we want
Surrendering to God is both the easiest and most difficult thing to
do
Easy because once you've let go, you tend not to worry about it
again
Difficult because you're used to fighting
But how long can you carry the burden for?
God sees your dragging your feet
Even if it's on the right path

Trust God
There are always replacements
To lift you
To guide you
To reach your potential
God protects you
So let go
Of what you can't control
Follow Him
God lights the way
Even when we think we're in darkness
Sometimes the weight of your heart is heavy in your hands
But light in God's
So why not give it up?
Be at peace with yourself
You can face tomorrow

Tears

When God puts a tear in your eye, it's because He wants to put a
rainbow in your heart
His blessings are the pot of gold

Heaven Opens

When you cry, you're washing God's feet with your tears
Maybe that's why the Heavens open
To tell you that He hears
We think that Heaven is so far away from here
But God's ability to respond always proves that He's near
He's sitting on the edge of His throne to peer
Waiting for you to lift your head up

Cry to God

I cried to God about it because I couldn't explain it to anyone else
Emotionally pressed
I started to think less of myself
Talking to God about it is the only way to make sense of anything
Sometimes prayer is the only way to progress through stress
Sometimes I don't know if I'm the object
Or the subject
But I take steps nevertheless
I set out to express myself
Especially when there's an emotional excess
When things get intense
Talking to God is the only defence
It gives me a chance to reflect
To assess the situation
Sometimes the distress is immense
When I'm feeling tense
Support is scarce
But I can't suppress my feelings either
Mind, heart, and soul protest against it
But sometimes things don't work out how we expect
So I reject it entirely
I don't want to waste my breath
So I talked to God
Because I know I won't regret it

Redundancy Prayer

Dear God,
Thank you for making me redundant
Once again you've reminded me that no job title or position is a
reflection of my self-worth
You've reminded me that social status is exactly that—it's social
Something for people to perceive you as being
Thank you for reminding me that life is uncertain
Nothing is stable, especially your job
Above everything, it reminds me that before I am anything
I am first and foremost your servant
Everything is secondary to that
I can only be a teacher for so long
Now it's time for me to learn some lessons
I'll count my blessings
The problem is I always lose count
Because there's countless times that you've been there for me
I'll ask for your guidance on this path
I ask for directions even though I know all roads lead to you
Even if they take a longer route
You've reminded me that prayer is more important than a payslip
You've reminded me that no insurance is better than your
reassurance
You've reminded me that your glory, your grace and gaze are more
important than the so-called glamour of a successful life

Find

When you go through something hard and wonder where God is
Remember that the teacher is always silent during the test
So try your best
Get everything off your chest
Because next time God sees you, you'll be differently dressed
God's always got a plan, so don't second guess
Don't lose sight of life's quest
Relax and rest
Don't stress
Give life its zest
Make God impressed
For being thankful for all He has blessed

Footsteps

Don't ask God to guide your footsteps
If you're not willing to move your feet
God has His own rhythm; you just must walk along to the beat
Don't ask God to give you the sun
If you can't handle the heat
Don't ask God to help you start
If you don't plan to complete

Surrender

Have you ever given something to God and God gave it right back
with a note saying, "You need to learn from that"?
Have you ever been ashamed that you can't see what God is
getting at?
Have you ever needed a hardhat for your blessings?
They fall down so hard that you can't even look at them

Trust the Process

Trust the process
The waiting
Everything in between
Trust the process
You're blessed
Navigate life like a game of chess
It can seem like a mess
But trust the process
Don't let it stress you out
Assess situations
Confess it to yourself
The process might distress you
But don't digress
Trust the process
Let it impress you

It'll help you progress
Be a success
Just trust the process

Correction

Sometimes the struggle is correction
With divine intervention
To get direction
For your own protection
So the lessons can be learnt
The struggle makes you special
Because you give it attention

Strength

Inner strength reveals itself at unlikely moments
The times you think that you've broken
Are when you get the closest
To do nothing but focus
The moment becomes frozen
Sometimes you must hit the lowest point
To notice
That you are open
Although the journey is long, you must appreciate the slowness
Otherwise those moments would be stolen
To be a component
Of condolence
Those golden moments are for atonement

Empowered

I'd rather be empowered instead of frightened
The experience is heightened
It makes you feel enlightened
Because you use your own guidance
The answers are found in silence

Disrupt

God will wreck your plans
Before they wreck you
That's how He checks in on you

God disrupts your entire life to talk to you
To take a walk with you

We will always fall short when we walk with God
But His grace is with us in the long run

Preparation

God is preparing you for more
Opening up different doors
More than you asked for
More than ever before

Spiritual Stamina

Develop spiritual stamina so when a problem occurs, we don't
react out of emotion
But out of wisdom
Where we find our frequency and rhythm
So that we see the vision
It's the best way to decide
Without the criticism
Without the cynicism
So that you're full of optimism

Strongest Warriors

They say that God gives His greatest battles to His strongest
warriors
I believe that
I can see that
Because God's got me on speed dial

Sometimes I'm tired of being the strong one
Can't you pick another?
Let someone else deal with the lessons and the bother
Fighters get tired too
They put their bodyweight on letting through
I know it's not our energy
It's His
But it's taken years
Things aren't always as they appear
I've learnt skills
But it's brought me to tears
They see with their eyes but don't hear with their ears
So it's just me and my sins
While God pulls His strings
But I feel it in my limbs
Especially when I go out on a limb
For Him
You have to have the will to win
But I'm still here singing my hymns
All glory to Him

Spiritual Training

Spiritual Training

Spiritual training is the hardest education
Because getting older doesn't mean elevation
Time changes expectations
Without explanations
There are lots of fluctuations
With no graduation
The only motivation is soul navigation
It's under constant observation and regulation
So, you can have revelations
That give you salvation
That is the ultimate transformation
To be God's manifestation

Grace

Grace

Sometimes a moment of grace can become a revelation

Mould

When God is moulding you
There is no room for someone else's hand
When you're a part of God's band
It doesn't matter who is a fan

God's Hands

God's hands are invisible
Sometimes people mistake that for inactive
But it depends how proactive you are
To determine the interaction
God is reactive to your actions
So if you're passive, how do you expect that to build traction?
God is adaptive
So when you're distracted
God can't be as expansive as He could be on your blessings

Imprint

God gave you a fingerprint that no one else has
So you can leave an imprint that no one else can
Over your lifespan

Pleasure

God does what pleases Him
Not what pleases you
He might give you something just to appease you
So you're not disappointed

Blameless

Dear God,
I am sorry I blame you
It's the easiest thing to do when you're frustrated
It's easier to question you when I can't find the answers
I know I'm supposed to give my burdens onto You
But when I try to
I'm left wondering, what am I supposed to do?
I'm waiting on You
I hope you're waiting on me
While I gather my thoughts and prepare myself for the next
opportunity
When I look at You
The highest version of me is reflecting back at me
I see what I am and so much more
All the potential
The true me
The real me
All of me

Silent Prayer

Pray for silence in your soul
It will drown out the noise of the mind
And amplify your heart

Quality Control

A bad day for your ego is a great day for your soul
It ensures quality control

God is Good

God is good
Especially when your prayers aren't answered
Your heart feels battered
But if everything went your way, then your ego would be flattered
When you ask for something and don't get it, God's reminding
you of your manners
You are a student of life, but God is the Master
Instead, appreciate the times that you've been pampered
So when your soul feels scattered
You didn't get what you wanted because you're living by God's
standards

Blessings in Disguise

We call them blessings in disguise
But aren't they just blessings?
But we're not looking right

Sometimes we underestimate our blessings
We cannot comprehend the gravity of God's grace
How it can weigh heavy and yet keep our soul light?

Miracles

You are a magnet for miracles
Miracles change your perception
Because a miracle is the exception to the rule
It's met with a different reception
There's lot of misconceptions
Until you learn the lesson
It's worth a mention
It only asks one question: How?
The tension brings attention
It forms a new impression

Abundance

Faith and Grace create abundance
They are a reminder that better things are coming
They create a compass
That does itself justice

Meet

God meets you where you're at
Not where you think you are
God helps you look ahead
God gives you intense preparation
To represent Him

Lonely Place

God meets you in your lonely place
To touch base with you
All you need to do is wait

God isolates you so you can get yourself together
It can seem that you've lost your people
But you're worth more
That space allowed you to unearth yourself

You

You
The instrument of God
How dare you let them silence your music
Like that melody hasn't been seen and heard centuries ago
Waiting an eternity to be listened to
Step into the most empowered version of yourself
Feel how sacred and divine that space is
The presence of silence Is not the absence of God

Put Myself Out There

I put myself out there
God put me back
Telling me I don't need to do that
So He took the flack
Gave me a knack to figuring things out
It was never what I lacked
It was more about my track
Off-beaten
Which was a comeback to myself

God's Plan

God has a perfect plan
One that unfolds for us every day
With our every step
Every breath
A door you didn't see before
Sometimes God subtracts
Sometimes God adds
Someone or something to your life
Once a purpose of anything is served—it stops
God ends things
To begin something else
God hears you
Even if you're not listening
God does things in His way
Not yours
Happiness might not be with people you think
God looks for you
Even if you don't see Him
When God leaves you alone in the dark
It's to remind you that He is the light
To guide you
To inspire you
Let God rearrange things
Change things for the better

Count on God

You'll lose count of how many times He's been there for you

Sometimes you have to rely on your faith

Instead of facts

We encounter problems

To have enough wisdom for the solution

God is constant

So don't be inconsistent

Bump

Dear God
There are too many mothers without babies
Too many empty stomachs
Too many overflowing hearts
Too many people that do everything right and somehow still get
it wrong
Too many women have been called every name under the sun
But *Mum*
Too many people want to hear footsteps, not their heart beating
like a drum
Too many people humming nursery rhymes with no one to sing to
Too many women anticipating pain but feeling numb
Too much pressure for kids to be added into the marriage sum
Too many women rubbing their stomachs because of the absence
of a bump

Catch

God has caught me more times than the ground has
Even when I've hit rock bottom
So forget the problems
Get to God—full throttle

Provide

God will provide and keep you strong
Whether you are right or wrong
He was with you all along
When you don't fit in anywhere else, in His heart you belong
All along

Truth

God's Dream

God created you
You are His dream come true

Expression

You are an expression of God
A question
That became God's confession
With discretion
To leave an impression on the world
You are Heaven's obsession

Pronunciation

Every time someone pronounces your name correctly
We consider it praising God
Because it's nothing short of a miracle
Pronouncing it again and again
A name should melt like caramel
But certain syllables are critical
Which makes it difficult
It seems minimal
But names are mystical
Mythical
Hearing your name makes you visible

Cuckoo Clock

God is in your heart the way a cuckoo is in a clock
Regular reminders of His presence
But He protected Himself by putting it in a ribcage
Put the ribcage in a body
Pour the soul in a body
And asked, *Do you still hear me?*
With all these layers of protection and disguise
Do you still feel me?
Maya Angelou knew why the caged bird sings
Because the bottom of its wings brushed the depths of her
intuition, asking her to pay attention
But did we listen?
We tune in and out like a pendulum
Say we're listening but we're swung back to the other side again
But still it moves
We make notes from the inner note
So our heart opens and closes
Leaning forward and backward
That's why it hangs on the wall
The chambers to our heart
The trap door that releases you
Strike like a heartbeat
A musical melody
So you tune in
Let it echo through your energy
Vibrate in a different frequency

Count

Count on God
And you'll never lose count

Mystery

We know God works in mysterious ways
But sometimes we want clarity
We need familiarity

Sarcasm

Everyone prays in their own language and there isn't a language
that God doesn't understand
Except maybe sarcasm
Even then
He'll call your bluff

God is not a vending machine

God is not a vending machine
To bend to your will
It's never ending
God can lend a hand
Help you mend
He'll send blessings
As a way of tending to you
Defending you
While you depend on Him
It's mind-bending

Enlightenment

Enlightenment is when a wave realised it's the ocean
Enlightenment is when magic is not in a potion
But in devotion

Gratitude

I thank You today
For the old trees with the new leaves
And the dreamy sky
It is all eternal
On days like today when life asks you to live
It's easy to say yes
To say it with your whole chest
Whole heart
In each breath
Today feels like a start
A new beginning
Of life and love
With your protection
It is all You
So you might as well live
Life doesn't hurry
It's waiting for You

Holy Rebel

I am a holy rebel
All bells and whistles
Dwelling on life
Coming out of my shell
Pebble skimming
I am raw
Sentimental and vulnerable
Liberated

You are waiting for you

You are waiting for you
Feeling like you're at a crossroads within yourself
You are waiting for you
Waiting for the red light to turn green
So you can cross the street
Stroll to your success
Wander along
Take it all in
The trek was to get to this place
You are your ride and die
Inner drive breaking through
You are waiting for you
Making moves in strides
You are waiting for you

Inconvenience

I want to die without being an inconvenience to others
Not to my sisters or my brother
Not to my father or my mother
I want to die knowing that I appreciated my life and all its colours
We all know our days are numbered

Rest in God

I don't want to rest in peace
I want to rest in God
To turn up at Heaven's gates and tell Him
I'm done

You

This is the moment of no return
The decision has already been made
You are in God's world
Everything will happen and it will all be unbelievable

About Atmosphere Press

Founded in 2015, Atmosphere Press was built on the principles of Honesty, Transparency, Professionalism, Kindness, and Making Your Book Awesome. As an ethical and author-friendly hybrid press, we stay true to that founding mission today.

If you're a reader, enter our giveaway for a free book here:

SCAN TO ENTER
BOOK GIVEAWAY

If you're a writer, submit your manuscript for consideration here:

SCAN TO SUBMIT
MANUSCRIPT

And always feel free to visit Atmosphere Press and our authors online at atmospherepress.com. See you there soon!

About the Author

I have an MA in Creative Writing and a BA in English Literature & Creative Writing. I have been writing and performing poetry for over nine years. I was a member of Apples and Snakes The Writing Room. My work has been published in the *London Spoken Word Anthology 2015-2016* by Gug Press, *Typishly*, Minerva Rising Press, *From Whispers to Roars*, *KYSO Flash*, Ghost City Press, San Fedele Press, Starfeather Publishing, Poets Choice, *The Road to Nowhere*, *DominAsian* magazine and *Brownies Verse*. I have two poetry collections, *Impression* and *For the Moment*, which is published by Atmosphere Press. I am one of the winners of the Art Fund Prize 2023 where my poem "Triggered" was displayed on billboards throughout the UK. I have co-authored *Transform From an Individual to an Entity* with Christoph Jenkins, head of The Poet Life. My debut play *Good Mourning* was showcased at the Hounslow Arts Centre.

www.ingramcontent.com/pod-product-compliance
Lightning Source LLC
Chambersburg PA
CBHW020722160726
47993CB00006B/2312